HISTORICAL   SERIES

FACET fb BOOKS

HISTORICAL SERIES — 9

(American Church)

Richard C. Wolf, Editor

The American Religious Depression 1925-1935

by ROBERT T. HANDY

FORTRESS PRESS   PHILADELPHIA

This study was originally published as "The American Religious Depression, 1925–1935" in *Church History,* XXIX (1960), 3-16, and is reprinted by arrangement with the author and the publisher.

Published by Fortress Press, 1968

INTRODUCTION ©1968 BY FORTRESS PRESS

Library of Congress Catalog Card Number 68-31338

217D68   Printed in U.S.A.   1-3048

Introduction

THE DEGREE of correlation and interplay between religion and the culture in which that religion finds expression has always intrigued church historians and, more recently, sociologists of religion.

To what extent does the culture affect the expression of religious belief? To what degree do religious ideals mold the patterns of culture? How essential to the perpetuation of the culture is religion and vice versa? Where are the limits beyond which the impact of religion on culture, or of culture on religion, cannot go without effecting some measure of damage to one or both, or to the relationship between them? How far may religion become acculturized and yet retain its integrity as religion? To what extent can any culture be said to be religious or more precisely "Christian"? These, and related questions, mark the trail as church historians and sociologists of religion endeavor to follow the intricate patterns of correlation and interplay.

Probably nowhere else are the patterns more complex and intricate than in the United States where the separation of state and church has set both culture and religion free from arbitrary and forcible control from outside or from within the relationship. Here neither state nor church has power to dictate to or control the other. The result has been a more flexible relationship and a more varied interplay than has been possible in situations where either the state or the church has been in a position to exert control.

The interpretations of the relationships of religion and culture in the United States have varied widely.

Secular historians to a very large extent have tended to allot a relatively limited amount of attention and significance to the place and role of the religious factor in comparison with political, diplomatic, military, economic, demographic, and other dimensions. Even those historians who have specialized in what is known as the cultural interpretation of American history have manifested this tendency to a greater or lesser degree.

Church historians employ a variety of interpretations, most of which fall, somewhat loosely, within four major general types.

First are the church historians who treat the history of the religious community as though it were isolated from, unrelated to, unconnected with, and not influenced by the surrounding culture. Such church historians frequently deal almost solely with the story of the organized church bodies and agencies, making only minimal reference, if any, to extra-ecclesiastical issues, involvements, and impacts.

Second are those historians who give religion a quite definitive role, at times a determinative role, in the formation of American culture. The claims that these historians make in behalf of the religious factor are at times so enthusiastic and sweeping as to raise some doubt about the validity of their claims and to lead the reader to inquire whether they may not be somewhat overdoing the significance of the religious factor with a concomitant underestimate of the part played by non-religious factors.

The third group of church historians works out of a well-established philosophy of church history which holds that religious organizations, groups, and movements show a manifest tendency to follow patterns already established or in process of being established within the culture. Initially, the outworking of this philosophy of church history seems rather attractive as an explanation of the life of the religious community in America. But upon closer scrutiny it proves to have serious drawbacks. First, it almost precludes the possibility of the religious forces being at any time the primary or initiating impulse in cultural modification and formulation. Second, it not infrequently requires the excision of segments of both cultural and religious history which, unfortunately for the historians' thesis, do not fit aptly into their descriptive scheme.

Lastly, there are those church historians, and their numbers are increasing, who view the relation between religion and culture in America as a steadily changing, almost kaleidoscopic pattern of interplay in which each side of the equation plays its own role, exerts its own influence, creates its own effects, and makes its own contribution in a generally beneficial symbiotic relationship. Such a "sitting loose in the saddle" approach is not conducive to the kind of neat spelling out of the historical narrative which is possible under the other types of interpretation we have mentioned, but it does permit the historian to approach each epoch, period, and event with freedom and openness. These historians are able to hold in balance what may seem to be mutually contradictory positions and relations of religion and culture and thus observe the long-range outworking of the interplay of these contesting elements. Similarly, the historian does not have to try to explain away or rationalize the "gray," clouded, and indistinct portions of his story. He is free to confess that certain areas are elusive or difficult to explain; that there are areas in which the elements of change, surprise, mutation, or even cataclysm must be reckoned with as phenomena of major importance.

Frequently the periods of history in which the correlation and interplay of religion and culture are most difficult to decipher prove to be among the more important segments of the story of their relationship, for more often than not they emerge as transition periods marking the end of one phase and the beginning of another.

The years between the stock market crash of 1929 and the onset of World War II constitute such a period. The patterns of interplay between religion and culture in these years seem very diffuse and somewhat chaotic. They appear to run counter to predictable patterns which had heretofore marked the relationship. At points, the economic and social turmoil which marked the "Great Depression" apparently had important impact upon the life and work of the churches; at other points the religious forces seemed to go their own way regardless of the potential hindrances and problems posed by prevailing economic and social conditions. Similarly, at certain points religious insights played a considerable role in trying to meet the critical societal situation, while at other points they seemed to have little or no influence.

There was a religious depression in these years of the massive economic depression, but church historians and sociologists of religion who have tried to draw a close parallel between the two depressions have been frustrated by a wealth of evidence that a direct and intimate correlation simply will not hold up. The religious depression cannot be explained solely, or even predominantly, as the consequence of the economic and social turmoil in the surrounding culture.

Professor Handy aptly pinpoints the cause of this inability to establish a close correlation. The difficulty lies in the tendency to seek too close and too immediate an interplay. He rightly distinguishes between the two depressions, pointing out that the religious depression began in the middle 1920's and was well under way when it was given added impetus by the economic collapse which dealt an "added blow to an American Protestantism already seriously weakened." The economic and social problems of the 1930's augmented problems with which American Protestantism in particular had already been wrestling in the 1920's.

The combined impact of the two depressions, religious and economic, made the period between 1925 and 1935 a time of religious transition and created a set of circumstances out of which a new religious situation emerged in the United States. Protestantism was no longer "the American religion." Liberal, optimistic theological positions had undergone a sobering reappraisal which tended to make them somewhat more "realistic," to use Reinhold Niebuhr's terminology. Thus, by the end of World War II American Christianity stood at the opening of a new period of potential interaction between religion and culture. Many of the old rules and patterns were going or gone. Not a few of the older explications of the relationships were passé. The ensuing years have seen the slow development of new patterns of correlation and interplay between culture and religion, patterns which many segments of the religious community have found challenging and exciting.

Professor Robert T. Handy joined the faculty of Union Theological Seminary in 1950 and has been Professor of Church History since 1959. He has concentrated his study on the history of American Christianity, with special emphasis on twentieth-century American Protestantism. His study of "The American Religious Depression, 1925–1935" (the Presidential Address before the American Society of Church History, December 29, 1959) emerges out of the core of his area of greatest competence and perception. It is consequently solidly grounded in wide-ranging research, yet its interpretations and conclusions are both exciting and helpful as American Christians view themselves, their ecclesiastical systems and bodies, and the surrounding culture and strive to gain some preview of what may lie ahead.

RICHARD C. WOLF

The Divinity School
Vanderbilt University
Nashville, Tennessee
June, 1968

THE AMERICAN RELIGIOUS DEPRESSION

1925 – 1935

"IT is too early to assess the impact of the Great Depression upon American Protestantism," wrote Robert Moats Miller in his study of American Protestantism and social issues in the period between the world wars.[1] No doubt it is still too early for any overall assessment, yet it is becoming steadily clearer that American religion passed through an important transition in the depression period. If we are to gain a fuller understanding of developments in American Christianity since the 1930's, then serious attention needs to be given to that bleak period. Inasmuch as our understanding of times long past are significantly influenced by our definitions of the present situation, attempts to deal with that particular period of crisis in our recent past may help us more adequately to see the whole story of American religion in better perspective. Furthermore, a number of recent dissertations, articles, and books have dealt in whole or in part with the period between the wars; they provide guidance for handling the vast array of sources relevant for an understanding of religion in the depression, supply material for at least preliminary interpretations, and point to the need for further analysis. This study is one effort to suggest some interpretative guidelines for further exploration into an important topic.

[1] *American Protestantism and Social Issues, 1919–1939* (Chapel Hill: University of North Carolina Press, 1958), p. 63.

I

In approaching the problem, it is important to distinguish between the economic depression of the 1930's and what may be called the religious depression. That there was an intimate relationship between them seems beyond doubt, yet they are also distinguishable phenomena. William Kelly Wright, Professor of Philosophy at Dartmouth College, writing in the heart of the depression period, declared that "today we are passing through a period of religious depression not less severe than the concomitant moral and economic depression."[2] Some months before the stock market crash of October, 1929, William L. Sullivan, a Unitarian writer, prepared an article entitled "Our Spiritual Destitution" in which he noted that the religion of his day was "timorous, unimaginative, quick with comment upon the contemporaneous, but unable in the authentic manner of its great tradition to judge the contemporaneous by categories that are eternal."[3] The effects of religious depression began to be felt by the middle 1920's within Protestantism, then the dominant and of course numerically the largest of the three overall religious groupings, Protestant, Roman Catholic, and Jewish, into which American religion is familiarly, though too simply, cast.

One sensitive indicator of a religion's vitality is its missionary program. By the middle of the third decade of the present century, Protestantism was becoming aware of a serious decline in missionary enthusiasm and conviction. At the 1926 meeting of the Foreign Missions Conference of North America, there was evident discouragement on the part of missionary leaders concerning the apathy of local churches toward the cause of missions.[4] Even after the disastrous effects of the economic de-

[2] "The Recovery of the Religious Sentiment," in *Contemporary American Theology: Theological Autobiographies,* ed. Vergilius Ferm (2 vols.; New York: Round Table Press, 1932–33), II, 367.

[3] *Atlantic Monthly,* CXLIII (January–June, 1929), 378.

[4] Fennell P. Turner and Frank Knight Sanders (eds.), *The Foreign Missions Conference of North America . . . 1926* (New York: Foreign Missions Conference, 1926), pp. 125-47.

pression had overtaken the missions boards, there was clear recognition that the problem was much more than financial, and that it had predated the economic crises. "However, we all know that this is not a sufficient explanation of what was happening on the home base," Edmund B. Chafee reported in 1934. He continued: "Interest in missions was waning before the depression. All through the decade of the 1920's the foreign missionary enterprise was being questioned and it was failing to attract the vigorous support which it formerly enjoyed."[5] In his sociological study of religion in the economic depression, Samuel C. Kincheloe reported that "even before the depression, missionary funds had begun to decrease."[6] Examination of the income figures of the major mission boards for the later 1920's reveals an irregular pattern but with a generally declining trend —and this in a period of booming prosperity![7] In an article entitled "The Decline of American Protestantism," Charles Stelzle in 1930 reported that according to the United Stewardship Council, per capita gifts for benevolence fell from $5.57 in 1921 to $3.43 in 1929.[8]

There was also a decline in the missionary force in these same years. The number of foreign missionaries in 1929 was less by 4.7 per cent than that for 1923.[9] The steadily waning interest of young people in responding to the missionary challenge was a source of concern at the 1929 meeting of the Foreign Missions Conference of North America, at which it was reported that though 2700 students had volunteered for foreign service in 1920, only 252 had offered themselves in

[5] "Some Conditions in North America that Affect Foreign Missions," in Leslie B. Moss and Mabel H. Brown (eds.), *The Foreign Missions Conference of North America . . . 1934* (New York: Foreign Missions Conference, 1934), p. 148.

[6] *Research Memorandum on Religion in the Depression,* Bulletin 33 (New York: Social Science Research Council, 1937), p. 51.

[7] Based on a study of the figures by the Rev. Donald A. Crosby, whose assistance in the research for this study I acknowledge with thanks.

[8] *Current History,* XXXIII (October, 1930), 25.

[9] C. Luther Fry, "Changes in Religious Organizations," in *Recent Social Trends* (2 vols.; New York: McGraw-Hill Book Co., 1933), II, 1046.

1928.[10] The decline of the missionary force for China was especially perplexing to missionary leaders, and led Albert W. Beaven to make a statement in 1928 that was in a strange way more prophetic than he could know. "What an absurdity if after one hundred years of service," he exclaimed, "after building up in China $90,000,000 of missionary investments in terms of helpfulness, we were to abandon it, withdrawing our Christian representatives, forsaking the whole enterprise, while at the very same time Russia with all the questionable principles she stands for is eager to offer the Orient men, counsel, money and moral backing."[11] It was the decline in missionary interest that led to the Laymen's Foreign Missions Inquiry in the early 1930's, which itself reflected a questioning of familiar missionary emphases within Protestantism.[12]

The home missions movement also felt the pinch of declining interest and diminishing funds before 1929. Nearly two years before the crash, the executive secretary of the Home Missions Council said:

> Almost all major denominations are now in a period of financial stringency in the conduct of mission work. We are in the days of failing budgets. There has been more or less retrenchment all along the line, and new work has been for several years practically at a standstill.[13]

On the rural church scene there was clear evidence of decline before 1929, both in terms of benevolence contributions and the attendance at services of resident members.[14]

---

[10] Stanley High, "The Need for Youth," in Leslie B. Moss (ed.), *The Foreign Missions Conference of North America . . . 1929* (New York: Foreign Missions Conference, 1929), p. 152.

[11] "What the Church Has to Say to Business Men About Foreign Missions," in Leslie B. Moss (ed.), *The Foreign Missions Conference of North America . . . 1928* (New York: Foreign Missions Conference, 1928), p. 85.

[12] [A study made under Baptist, Congregational, Dutch Reformed, Episcopal, Methodist, and Presbyterian auspices. *Rethinking Missions* (New York: Harper & Bros., 1932).—Ed.]

[13] *Home Missions Council Annual Report . . . 1928* (New York: Home Missions Council, 1928), p. 80.

[14] Kincheloe, *Research Memorandum,* pp. 133 f.

The problem of falling attendance was not limited to the rural scene, of course, for churches in all areas reported difficulties in maintaining attendance levels. A general trend toward the dropping of traditional Sunday evening services, especially in the cities, was observed.[15] Decline in Sunday school enrollment was also evident; C. Luther Fry found in 1930 that "the proportion of young people attending church schools is greater today than in 1906, but less than in 1916."[16] Attempts to plot an "evangelistic index line" for a number of major denominations point to a sharp downturn in the winning of converts and the reception of new members in the 1920's.[17] A somewhat less tangible evidence of Protestant decline was the lowered status of ministers. Paul A. Carter has pointed out that the ministry sank low in public esteem in this period; he quotes a minister of that time who declared that it was "a fairly safe generalization to say that no profession of men is so thoroughly empty of dignity and grace as that of the Protestant minister today."[18]

Many observers have called attention to the slump which overtook the social gospel in the later 1920's; it is referred to in the very title of Carter's book, *The Decline and Revival of the Social Gospel.* But in his recent examination of the period, Robert Moats Miller has found that "social Christianity continued to burn bright enough to warrant future historians in using slightly less somber hues in painting their pictures of the social attitudes of American Protestantism in the Prosperity Decade."[19] The apparent contradiction may be resolved by con-

[15] *Ibid.,* p. 51; *Recent Social Trends,* II, 1055.

[16] *The U.S. Looks At Its Churches* (New York: Institute of Social and Religious Research, 1930), p. 58.

[17] H. C. Weber, *Evangelism: A Graphic Survey* (New York: Macmillan Co., 1929), pp. 181 f. I have had the opportunity of seeing charts plotting the "evangelistic index" and summarizing membership trends prepared by the Rev. Harold Edgar Martin; in general they all show decline beginning about 1925 and not showing significant upturn until the middle 1930's.

[18] *The Decline and Revival of the Social Gospel: Social and Political Liberalism in American Protestant Churches, 1920–1940* (Ithaca: Cornell University Press, 1954), p. 70, quoting Ellis J. Hough, "Terrors of the Protestant Ministry," *Presbyterian Advance,* XL (January 30, 1930), 18.

[19] *American Protestantism and Social Issues,* p. 47.

cluding that though proportionately the social emphasis remained strong, the social gospel movement as a whole was caught in Protestantism's overall decline.

Some of the keenest observers of the religious life of the late 1920's recognized that they were in some kind of a religious depression. For example, the Episcopal Bishop of Central New York, Charles Fiske, was convinced in 1928 that he had "evidence of a sad disintegration of American Protestantism."[20] And in his first book, published in 1927, Reinhold Niebuhr remarked that "a psychology of defeat, of which both fundamentalism and modernism are symptoms, has gripped the forces of religion."[21] At least part of the reason for the decline was the penetration into the churches of the prevailing mood of the 1920's. For Protestantism was deeply affected by the general disillusionment of the postwar decade. During the war itself, the American people, with the vigorous support of most religious leaders, maintained a spirit of high optimism. But the tide turned swiftly. As Arthur S. Link has recently reminded us, "the 1920's were a period made almost unique by an extraordinary reaction against idealism and reform."[22] The rapid subsidence of the war spirit, so Walter M. Horton observed in a book written in 1929 but published the following year, led "to a wave of spiritual depression and religious skepticism, widespread and devastating."[23] Protestantism felt the corrosive effects of disillusionment at the very beginning of the decade, for the collapse of the grandiose Interchurch World Movement in 1920 was at least in part caused by the swift change in mood. Winthrop S. Hudson has summarized the swift decline of Protestantism in a vivid way:

[20] *The Confessions of a Puzzled Parson* (New York: Charles Scribner's Sons, 1928), p. 191.
[21] *Does Civilization Need Religion? A Study in the Social Resources and Limitations of Religion in Modern Life* (New York: Macmillan Co., 1927), p. 2.
[22] "What Happened to the Progressive Movement in the 1920's," *American Historical Review*, LXIV (1959), 833. See also the perceptive article by Henry F. May, "Shifting Perspectives in the 1920's," *Mississippi Valley Historical Review*, XLIII (1956), 405-27.
[23] *Theism and the Modern Mood* (New York: Harper & Bros., 1930), p. 6.

Nothing is more striking than the astonishing reversal in the position occupied by the churches and the role played by religion in American life which took place before the new century was well under way. By the nineteen twenties, the contagious enthusiasm which had been poured into the Student Volunteer Movement, the Sunday School Movement, the Men and Religion Forward Movement, the Laymen's Missionary Movement, the Interchurch World Movement, and other organized activities of the churches had largely evaporated.[24]

As the decade wore on, scientism, behaviorism, and humanism became more conspicuous in the thought of the time. Religion was often viewed with a negative if not with a hostile eye. In his effort to state the case for "a promethean religion for the modern world," William Pepperell Montague declared in 1930 that "there is today a widespread and increasing belief that the minimum essentials of Christian supernaturalism . . . have been rendered antiquated, false, and absurd by our modern knowledge."[25] More extreme was Joseph Wood Krutch's pessimistic statement of "the modern temper" in 1929. Referring to such classic words as "Sin" and "Love," Krutch wrote that "all the capital letters in the composing-room cannot make the words more than that which they have become—shadows, as essentially unreal as some of the theological dogmas which have been completely forgotten."[26] Criticism of religion and the churches was expressed not only by men like Montague and Krutch, by H. L. Mencken and Sinclair Lewis, but also by many less well-known men. One opinion study showed that although about 78 per cent of the traditional views about Christianity published in 1905 were favorable and only 22 per cent were unfavorable, by 1930 the situation had almost reversed, so that 67 per cent of the opinions published were unfavorable.[27]

Protestantism was deeply penetrated by the disillusionment

[24] *The Great Tradition of the American Churches* (New York: Harper & Bros., 1953), p. 196.
[25] *Belief Unbound: A Promethean Religion for the Modern World* (New Haven: Yale University Press, 1930), p. 20.
[26] *The Modern Temper: A Study and a Confession* (New York: Harcourt, Brace & Co., 1929), pp. 191 f.
[27] Hornell Hart, "Changing Social Attitudes and Interests," in *Recent Social Trends*, I, 403.

of the time in part at least because of a long-standing identification of Protestantism with American culture which left the
churches quite exposed to cultural crosscurrents. The roots of
this identification go far back to the beginnings of American
history. As André Siegfried stated the matter in 1927:

> If we wish to understand the real sources of American inspiration,
> we must go back to the English Puritanism of the seventeenth
> century, for the civilization of the United States is essentially
> Protestant. Those who prefer other systems, such as Catholicism,
> for example, are considered bad Americans and are sure to be
> frowned on by the purists. Protestantism is the only national re-
> ligion, and to ignore that fact is to view the country from a false
> angle.

Siegfried was fully aware of the denominational nature of Protestantism, yet still insisted on his main point: "In order to
appreciate the influence of Protestantism in this confusion of
sects, we must not look at it as a group of organized churches,
for its strength lies in the fact that its spirit is national."[28]
Sidney E. Mead has recently shown that the fusion of Protestantism with Americanism was especially evident in the later
nineteenth century. He has suggested that "during the second
half of the nineteenth century there occurred a virtual identification of this denominational Protestantism with 'Americanism'
or 'the American way of life' and that we are still living with
some of the results of this ideological amalgamation of evangelical Protestantism with Americanism."[29] During and just
after World War I there was an intensification of this synthesis through an emphasis on "Christian Americanization," by
which was meant growth toward national democratic and spiritual ideals, of which the churches were the best custodians.[30]

---

[28] *America Comes of Age*, trans. H. H. Hemming and Doris Hemming
(New York: Harcourt, Brace & Co., 1927), pp. 33, 38 f.

[29] "American Protestantism Since the Civil War. I. From Denomina-
tionalism to Americanism," *Journal of Religion*, XXXVI (1956), 1. Reprinted in Sidney E. Mead, *The Lively Experiment* (New York: Harper
& Row, 1963).

[30] Cf. chap. iii, "Christian Americanization," of my *We Witness Together:
A History of Cooperative Home Missions* (New York: Friendship Press,
1956), pp. 64-82.

One feature of this identification was illustrated in the Lynds' comment following their 1925 study of "Middletown": "In theory, religious beliefs dominate all other activities in Middletown."[31]

The religious education movement, which was at the peak of its influence in the later 1920's, clearly illustrated the theme of the ideological amalgamation of religion and culture. Shailer Mathews pointed to its triumphs in 1927 by declaring that "it commands the same sort of enthusiastic following from idealistic young men and women as did sociology a generation ago. The most generally elected courses in theological seminaries, the greatest activity in churches are in its field." But Mathews warned religious educators that they were tending to neglect the church in their concern for education, insisting that "it is our privilege to teach young people that religion has some other task than that of making good citizens and good neighbors."[32] As H. Shelton Smith was later to document, many religious educators "sought to blend the democratic theory of education and the democratic theory of the Kingdom of God."[33]

In view of this identification, it was inevitable that Protestantism would be deeply and directly influenced by trends within the culture, and that many of them would be accepted and even blessed by the churches. In 1929 the self-styled "puzzled parson," Charles Fiske, indicated that he was not quite as puzzled as he claimed to be when he said:

> America has become almost hopelessly enamoured of a religion that is little more than a sanctified commercialism; it is hard in this day and this land to differentiate between religious aspiration and business prosperity. Our conception of God is that he is sort of a Magnified Rotarian. Sometimes, indeed, one wonders whether the social movement and the uplift in general have not become, among Protestants, a substitute for devotion; worse than that, a

---

[31] Robert S. Lynd and Helen Merrell Lynd, *Middletown: A Study in Contemporary American Culture* (New York: Harcourt, Brace & Co., 1929), p. 406.

[32] "Let Religious Education Beware!" *Christian Century,* XLIV (1927), 362.

[33] *Faith and Nurture* (New York: Charles Scribner's Sons, 1941), p. 41.

substitute for real religion. Efficiency has become the greatest of Christian virtues. I hope I may be forgiven a note of exaggeration that is necessary to make my meaning clear when I say that Protestantism, in America, seems to be degenerating into a sort of Babsonian cult, which cannot distinguish between what is offered to God and what is accomplished for the glory of America and the furtherance of business enterprise.[34]

Edwin Lewis of Drew University, reviewing in 1934 the course American Protestantism had taken during the previous twenty years, declared:

We borrowed our criteria of evaluation from the world about us —a world gone mad in its worship of mere size, a world that had set itself to create bigger ships, bigger aeroplanes, bigger locomotives, bigger buildings, bigger universities, bigger corporations, bigger banks, bigger everything—except men! . . . And we were guilty of the incredible folly of supposing that "Christ's church was of this world," to be judged by the world's standards, to be modeled on the world's ways, to walk in the world's procession, and to keep step to the crashing discord of its brazen shawms.[35]

In light of such identification with the culture, Protestantism could hardly avoid a share in the spiritual poverty of the time, or escape wholly from the spirit of disillusionment that swept American life in the 1920's. The American spiritual depression and the decline of Protestantism in the 1920's were intimately correlated.

It was on churches already seriously weakened, already in some decline, that the blow of economic depression fell. When the Lynds returned to Middletown ten years after their first study they found that

the city had been shaken for nearly six years by a catastrophe involving not only people's values, but in the case of many, their very existence. Unlike most socially generated catastrophes, in this case virtually nobody in the community had been cushioned against

---

[34] *Confessions of a Puzzled Parson,* p. 14.

[35] *A Christian Manifesto* (New York: Abingdon Press, 1934), p. 202.

the blow; the great knife of the depression had cut down impartially through the entire population, cleaving open the lives and hopes of rich as well as poor.[36]

The great knife of depression also cut deep into church life. "Outwardly the churches suffered along with the rest of the nation," wrote Robert M. Miller. "Memberships dropped, budgets were slashed, benevolent and missionary enterprises set adrift, ministers fired, and chapels closed. All this can be demonstrated statistically."[37] The evidence need not be summarized here, but a single illustration of the impact of depression may be in order. In 1927 Shailer Mathews had reported the triumph of religious education; less than ten years later, after depression had done its work, Adelaide Teague Case painted a dark picture.

What shall we say to Christian Education today? Obviously it is in distress. The machinery has broken down. All the denominational boards of education have suffered great losses. The International Council of Religious Education is struggling on with a greatly reduced staff and budget. The Religious Education Association is in abeyance, trying to maintain itself with a handful of volunteers who are holding it together in spite of a staggering debt. Training schools and departments of religious education in universities and seminaries are severely reduced in size; some of them have reorganized or disappeared. The professional leadership is discouraged; directors of religious education are transferring to social work or public education or joining the ranks of the unemployed.[38]

This illustration could be matched by pointing to many other aspects of the churches' programs. Hidden in such a flat statement as "twenty out of thirty-five leading denominations com-

[36] Robert S. Lynd and Helen Merrell Lynd, *Middletown in Transition: A Study in Cultural Conflicts* (New York: Harcourt, Brace & Co., 1937), p. 295.

[37] *American Protestantism and Social Issues*, p. 63.

[38] "Christian Education," in Samuel McCrea Cavert and Henry P. Van Dusen (eds.), *The Church Through Half a Century: Essays in Honor of William Adams Brown* (New York: Charles Scribner's Sons, 1936), pp. 243 f.

pared in 1934 had reduced their total expenditures by from thirty to fifty per cent and five over fifty per cent" are countless stories of struggles, discouragement, and tragedy.[39]

This approach to religion in the depression, to distinguish between religious and economic depressions, throws light on many aspects of religious life in the 1930's, but on the following three in particular. First, one of the persistent questions of the depression period was "Why no revival of religion?" Some religious leaders, reported Samuel Kincheloe, "actually hailed the depression with rejoicing since they had the idea that previous depressions had 'driven men to God' and felt that the time was overdue for men again to be reminded of the need to let the spiritual dominate the materialistic order."[40] At various times in the American past, depression and revival had been related, classically in 1857–1858. But when the distinction between religious and economic depression is made, it becomes clear that it was an already depressed Protestantism that was overtaken by the economic crisis. Without inner changes it was unable to deal with the needs of the time in a fresh and creative way. The changes that finally came did contribute to conspicuous currents of renewal, but only after the depression itself had passed.

Second, a significant aspect of the religious depression, perplexing to the major denominations, was the mushrooming of the newer and smaller religious groups, the sects. Detailed analyses of particular communities, such as Pope's study of Gastonia, the Lynds' probing of Middletown, and Boisen's samplings of several communities, all document the proliferation of the sects in the depression decade.[41] A number of observers have pointed out that many, probably a majority, of the supporters of sectarian movements were formerly adherents of

[39] H. Paul Douglass and Edmund deS. Brunner, *The Protestant Church as a Social Institution* (New York: Harper & Bros., 1935), p. 208.

[40] *Research Memorandum*, p. 1.

[41] Liston Pope, *Millhands and Preachers: A Study of Gastonia* (New Haven: Yale University Press, 1942), pp. 126, 128; *Middletown in Transition*, p. 297; Anton T. Boisen, "Religion and Hard Times," *Social Action*, V (March 15, 1939), 8-35.

the older and larger Protestant denominations. That the sects attracted many among the "disinherited" and economically depressed classes has been stated many times.[42] A significant but indirect factor in the rapid growth of the sects in the 1930's would seem to be the internal Protestant depression with its consequent lack of clarity and energy in the churches. Individuals won from older to newer religious bodies often indicated their dissatisfaction with the coldness and formality of the oldline churches.

Third, one of the major shifts of mood which was certainly speeded by the lash of depression was the somewhat precipitous decline of the evangelical liberal theology, which had been so conspicuous a part of Protestant life in the first quarter of the century. There were some signs of the internal disintegration of liberalism even before the first world war.[43] In 1925, Justin Wroe Nixon explained the liberal's dilemma in a forceful article in the *Atlantic*. While the liberals were fighting off the frontal attack of fundamentalism, he declared, they were inadvertently backing toward the humanist position; they were seriously embarrassed by the flank attack of the naturalists and humanists.[44] The latter claimed to speak for a scientifically- and naturalistically-minded age far better than the liberals, who were accused of clinging to an unsatisfactory and unstable compromise, could. By the early 1930's, liberals were finding it increasingly difficult, in terms of their optimistic orientation and idealistic heritage, to deal satisfactorily with the realities of depression, the rise of totalitarianism, and the resurgence of barbarism on the world scene. In his famous article of 1933, "After Liberalism—What?" John C. Bennett said emphatically:

> The most important fact about contemporary American theology is the disintegration of liberalism. Disintegration may seem too

[42] E.g., cf. Boisen, *loc. cit.*; Elmer T. Clark, *The Small Sects in America* (rev. ed.; New York: Abingdon-Cokesbury Press, 1949), pp. 16-20, 218 f., 230.

[43] Walter Marshall Horton, *Realistic Theology* (New York: Harper & Bros., 1934), p. 35.

[44] "The Evangelicals' Dilemma," *Atlantic Monthly,* CXXXVI (July–December, 1925), 368-74.

strong a word, but I am using it quite literally. It means that as a structure with a high degree of unity theological liberalism is coming to pieces. The liberal preacher has had a coherent pattern of theological assumptions in the background of his message. He has often had the kind of self-confidence which goes with the preaching of an orthodoxy, for liberalism has been a new orthodoxy in many circles. It is that coherent pattern of assumptions, that self-confidence, which are going. Now many of us are left with a feeling of theological homelessness.[45]

Into the vacuum new theological currents immediately flowed, as interpreters of European dialectical theologies appeared.[46] Benson Y. Landis could report in 1933 that "the economic crisis seems to be breeding a theology of crisis."[47] But one must not press too hard the relationship between the depression and the decline of liberalism. It was not the depression alone but the many crises of the 1930's which together weakened the liberal synthesis and made men receptive to new views. When the *Christian Century* published in 1939 its oft-quoted series of articles on "How My Mind Has Changed in This Decade," many of America's leading theologians told how the fateful events of the decade had led them to shift their position to a neo-liberalism if not a neo-orthodoxy. A characteristic expression of the impact of the decade on the liberals was penned by E. G. Homrighausen. "I saw evidences of man's lostness: the depression, the constant threat of war, the return to brutality on so vast a scale, the loss of the spiritual substance of life that alone gives society structure, the uncertainty and insecurity of life."[48]

Somewhat paradoxically—for the rise of the social gospel had been intimately related to the earlier success of theological liberalism—there was clearly a resurgence of the social gospel in the 1930's, despite the decay of liberalism. The works of

[45] *Christian Century*, L (1933), 1403.

[46] Cf. Sydney E. Ahlstrom, "Continental Influence on American Christian Thought Since World War I," *Church History*, XXVII (1958), 256-72.

[47] "Organized Religion," *American Journal of Sociology*, XXXVIII (July, 1932–May, 1933), 907.

[48] "Calm After Storm," *Christian Century*, LVI (1939), 479.

Paul A. Carter and Robert M. Miller, previously cited, document this resurgence of social concern abundantly; a hasty examination of denominational social pronouncements in the bleak decade provides convincing confirmation. Hornell Hart reported some years ago on this aspect of religion in the depression in these words:

> The most striking increase in religious discussion in magazines has been in the field of Christian ethics. *Readers' Guide* entries under this heading and under "Church and Social Problems," "Christian Socialism," and "Christian Sociology" increased from 17 per 100,000 in 1929 to 140 in 1932, and in 1941 they were still more than twice their 1929 level. The rise and recession of this curve is notably similar to the rise and decline in the amount of unemployment and to other indices of the economic depression.[49]

That there was something of a resurgence of the social gospel seems apparent, but on the whole the resurgence of social interest in the 1930's is perhaps more to be seen as related to a permanent contribution which the social gospel in its creative days earlier in the century had made to the larger Protestant world: a sensitivity to social issues and an awareness of social need. A Protestantism which had been alerted by such a vigorous social movement could not easily be callous to serious social need. Not a few of those who took leadership in movements to the theological right were also conspicuous for their continued attention to social thought and action.

II

I have argued that Protestantism entered the period of religious and economic depression as the dominant American religious tradition, closely identified with the culture. But Protestantism emerged from depression no longer in such a position; it was challenged by forces outside the Protestant churches and

[49] "Religion," *American Journal of Sociology,* XLVII (July, 1941—May, 1942), 894.

questioned by some within. Siegfried, who identified Protestantism as the national religion as late as 1927, saw the trend of the times:

> The worldliness of this Protestantism and its pretensions to be a national religion reserved for the privileged few have antagonized many of its followers as well as its adversaries. They feel that something is lacking, almost the spirit of religion itself; for the ultimate has been reduced until it embraces little more than ethics.[50]

And though the Lynds had indicated that *in theory* religious beliefs dominated all other activities in Middletown, they hastened to add that "actually, large regions of Middletown's life appear uncontrolled by them."[51] In this period, the vast rural reservoirs of Protestant strength were rather rapidly being outmatched by the flooding cities. The Protestantism that threw itself so strongly behind prohibition in the 1920's was one in which the rural tradition was still very strong. Indeed, prohibition itself was in one sense part of the struggle of country against city. The legislative superintendent of the Anti-Saloon League recognized in 1917 that the Eighteenth Amendment had to pass before 1920, for with reapportionment would come, as he put it, "forty new wet Congressmen . . . from the great wet centers with their rapidly increasing population."[52] The final failure of prohibition made it clearer to many Protestants that the familiar American culture in which they had flourished and with which they had been so closely identified was going. The comfortable identification with American cultural patterns no longer seemed so relevant or so helpful.

The beginnings of Protestant renewal, which Herbert Wallace Schneider notes as arising in the "dark 30's" and continuing as an "offensive which has grown steadily since then,"[53] developed

[50] *America Comes of Age,* p. 46.

[51] *Middletown,* p. 406.

[52] Wayne Wheeler, as quoted by Paul A. Carter in *The Decline and Revival of the Social Gospel,* p. 37.

[53] *Religion in Twentieth Century America* (Cambridge: Harvard University Press, 1952), p. 18.

in part as religious leaders challenged the identification of Protestantism with American culture and summoned the church to recover its own independent standing-ground. In 1935, Harry Emerson Fosdick preached the famous sermon in which he appealed to Protestants to go "beyond modernism." He exclaimed,

> And in that new enterprise the watchword will be not, Accommodate yourself to the prevailing culture! but, Stand out from it and challenge it! For this inescapable fact, which again and again in Christian history has called modernism to its senses, we face: we cannot harmonize Christ himself with modern culture. What Christ does to modern culture is to challenge it.[54]

And in that same year, to cite another example, appeared a book with the revealing title *The Church Against the World.* It vigorously protested the identification of the church with American culture. Francis P. Miller wrote: "The plain fact is that the domestication of the Protestant community in the United States within the framework of the national culture has progressed as far as in any western land. The degradation of the American Protestant church is as complete as the degradation of any other national Protestant church."[55] What the church should therefore do was stated by H. Richard Niebuhr in these words:

> We live, it is evident, in a time of hostility when the church is imperiled not only by an external worldliness but by one that has established itself within the Christian camp. Our position is inside a church which has been on the retreat and which has made compromises with the enemy in thought, in organization, and in discipline. Finally, our position is in the midst of that increasing group in the church which had heard the command to halt, to remind itself of its mission, and to await further orders.[56]

[54] "Beyond Modernism: A Sermon," *Christian Century,* LII (1935), 1552.
[55] H. Richard Niebuhr, Wilhelm Pauck, and Francis P. Miller, *The Church Against the World* (Chicago: Willett, Clark & Co., 1935), p. 102.
[56] *Ibid.,* pp. 1 f.

As James H. Smylie has analyzed the theological trend of a steadily enlarging group in American Protestantism, it was "a trend from an irrelevant attachment to society toward a relevant detachment to society without becoming irrelevantly detached from society."[57] The "Christ of culture" motif, which had long been of great significance in American Protestantism, was being challenged from within. From a widening circle of Protestants seeking to return again by one route or another to the independent sources of their faith, there came movements of renewal which marked the beginning of the end of the religious depression for Protestants. There were also other sources of renewal, but this one bears a special relation to our theme.

I have entitled this study the "American" religious depression because there was a nationally observable spiritual lethargy evident in the 1920's and 1930's, and because the then clearly dominant religious tradition of the country was in decline. Certainly both Judaism and Roman Catholicism were deeply affected by the economic depression; to what extent they were internally affected by spiritual depression the authorities on those bodies must say. Jewish congregations enjoyed a healthy growth in the 1926–36 decade, reporting a 13.7 per cent increase. Roman Catholicism also grew, but considerably more slowly than in the preceding ten-year period. The church had then reported an 18.3 per cent growth, which dropped to 7 per cent for 1926–1936.[58] Perhaps this change was influenced both by the cutting off of immigration and by the generally unfriendly attitude toward religion. But neither Judaism or Catholicism was embarrassed by too close identification with the surrounding culture, for both felt their minority situation rather keenly. When George N. Shuster wrote his widely-read work on the Catholic spirit in America in 1927, he began by noting that "twenty or thirty years ago ambition would have dictated silence about one's mere connection with what is termed

[57] "The American Protestant Churches and the Depression of the 1930's" (Th.M. Thesis, Princeton Theological Seminary, 1950), p. 125.

[58] Bureau of the Census, *Religious Bodies: 1936* (Washington: U.S. Government Printing Office, 1941), I, 51.

the Roman Church. Today prudence still seems to suggest keeping this matter under cover as fully as possible."[59] But during the depression years a significant change took place; Protestantism declined and lost its sense of being the national religion, while Roman Catholicism, reflecting advances made during and after the war years, consolidated by the National Catholic Welfare Conference, rather quickly became more visible on the American scene. It was less than fifteen years from the time that Shuster wrote the words just quoted that the popular historian Theodore Maynard made this claim:

> Protestantism—especially American Protestantism—is now so doctrinally decayed as to be incapable of offering any serious opposition to the sharp sword of the Spirit, as soon as we can make up our minds to use it. Except for isolated "fundamentalists,"— and these are pretty thoroughly discredited and without intellectual leadership—Catholicism could cut through Protestantism as through so much butter.[60]

The contrast between the two quotations dramatizes an important religious transition of the depression period. The upshot of that transition which focused in depression years, though it had been long in the making, was summarized by Will Herberg in his book, *Protestant–Catholic–Jew:*

> In net effect, Protestantism today no longer regards itself either as a religious movement sweeping the continent or as a national church representing the religious life of the people; Protestantism understands itself today primarily as one of the three religious communities in which twentieth century America has come to be divided.[61]

During the period of religious and economic depression, then, the "Protestant era" in America was brought to a close; Prot-

---

[59] *The Catholic Spirit in America* (New York: Lincoln MacVeagh, Dial Press, 1927), p. vii.

[60] *The Story of American Catholicism* (New York: Macmillan Co., 1941), p. 613.

[61] *Protestant–Catholic–Jew: An Essay in American Religious Sociology* (Garden City: Doubleday & Co., 1955), pp. 139 f.

estantism emerged no longer the "national religion." The test of depression was a severe one; it laid bare certain weaknesses in American Protestantism. But the repudiation of the virtual identification of Protestantism with American culture by an able and growing group of religious leaders freed many Protestants to recover in a fresh way their own heritages and their original sources of inspiration. The depression stimulated many Protestants to seek new and deeper understandings of their own religious heritage, though this "positive" contribution of the depression to religion could probably be appreciated only later. The years of religious and economic depression were years of significant transition for the American churches, for in that period trends long in the making were dramatically revealed, and developments important to the future became visible.

For Further Reading

MILLER, ROBERT M. *American Protestantism and Social Issues, 1919–1939*. Chapel Hill: University of North Carolina Press, 1958.

Research Memorandum on Religion in the Depression. Bulletin 33. New York: Social Science Research Council, 1937.

The U.S. Looks At Its Churches. New York: Institute of Social and Religious Research, 1930.

MEYER, DONALD B. *The Protestant Search for Political Realism, 1919–1941*. Berkeley and Los Angeles: University of California Press, 1960.

CARTER, PAUL A. *The Decline and Revival of the Social Gospel: Social and Political Liberalism in American Protestant Churches, 1920–1940*. Ithaca: Cornell University Press, 1954.

MAY, HENRY F. "Shifting Perspectives in the 1920's," *Mississippi Valley Historical Review*, XLIII (1956), 405-27.

HUDSON, WINTHROP S. *Religion in America*. New York: Charles Scribner's Sons, 1965.

MEAD, SIDNEY E. *The Lively Experiment*. New York: Harper & Row, 1963.

DOUGLASS, H. PAUL and EDMUND DES. BRUNNER. *The Protestant Church as a Social Institution*. New York: Harper & Bros., 1935.

SCHNEIDER, HERBERT W. *Religion in Twentieth Century America*. Cambridge: Harvard University Press, 1952.

NIEBUHR, H. RICHARD, WILHELM PAUCK, and FRANCIS P. MILLER. *The Church Against the World*. Chicago: Willett, Clark & Co., 1935.

Facet Books Already Published

Historical Series:

1. *Were Ancient Heresies Disguised Social Movements?*
   by A. H. M. Jones. 1966
2. *Popular Christianity and the Early Theologians*
   by H. J. Carpenter. 1966
3. *Tithing in the Early Church*
   by Lukas Vischer (translated by Robert C. Schultz). 1966
4. *Jerusalem and Rome*
   by Hans von Campenhausen and Henry Chadwick. 1966
5. *The Protestant Quest For A Christian America 1830–1930*
   by Robert T. Handy. 1967
6. *The Formation of the American Catholic Minority 1820–1860*
   by Thomas T. McAvoy. 1967
7. *A Critical Period In American Religion 1875–1900*
   by Arthur M. Schlesinger, Sr. 1967
8. *Images of Religion in America*
   by Jerald C. Brauer. 1967
9. *The American Religious Depression 1925–1935*
   by Robert T. Handy. 1968
10. *The Origins of Fundamentalism: Toward a Historical Interpretation*
    by Ernest R. Sandeen. 1968

Biblical Series:

1. *The Significance of the Bible for the Church*
   by Anders Nygren (translated by Carl Rasmussen). 1963
2. *The Sermon on the Mount*
   by Joachim Jeremias (translated by Norman Perrin). 1963
3. *The Old Testament in the New*
   by C. H. Dodd. 1963
4. *The Literary Impact of the Authorized Version*
   by C. S. Lewis. 1963
5. *The Meaning of Hope*
   by C. F. D. Moule. 1963

6. *Biblical Problems and Biblical Preaching*
   by C. K. Barrett.   1964
7. *The Genesis Accounts of Creation*
   by Claus Westermann (translated by Norman E. Wagner). 1964
8. *The Lord's Prayer*
   by Joachim Jeremias (translated by John Reumann).   1964
9. *Only to the House of Israel? Jesus and the Non-Jews*
   by T. W. Manson.   1964
10. *Jesus and the Wilderness Community at Qumran*
    by Ethelbert Stauffer (translated by Hans Spalteholz).   1964
11. *Corporate Personality in Ancient Israel*
    by H. Wheeler Robinson.   1964
12. *The Sacrifice of Christ*
    by C. F. D. Moule.   1964
13. *The Problem of the Historical Jesus*
    by Joachim Jeremias (translated by Norman Perrin).   1964
14. *A Primer of Old Testament Text Criticism*
    by D. R. Ap-Thomas.   1966
15. *The Bible and the Role of Women*
    by Krister Stendahl (translated by Emilie T. Sander).   1966
16. *Introduction to Pharisaism*
    by W. D. Davies.   1967
17. *Man and Nature in the New Testament*
    by C. F. D. Moule.   1967
18. *The Lord's Supper According to the New Testament*
    by Eduard Schweizer (translated by James M. Davis).   1967
19. *The Psalms: A Form-Critical Introduction*
    by Herman Gunkel (translated by Thomas Horner).   1967
20. *The Spirit-Paraclete in the Fourth Gospel*
    by Hans Windisch (translated by James W. Cox).   1968
21. *The Semitic Background of the term "Mystery" in the New Testament*
    by Raymond E. Brown, S.S.   1968

Social Ethics Series:

1. *Our Calling*
   by Einar Billing (translated by Conrad Bergendoff).   1965
2. *The World Situation*
   by Paul Tillich.   1965
3. *Politics as a Vocation*
   by Max Weber (translated by H. H. Gerth and C. Wright Mills).   1965

FACET fb BOOKS

brief treatments of major themes in social ethics, religious history, and the Bible, by leading scholars and teachers.

HISTORICAL SERIES (American Church)

edited by

Richard C. Wolf

Professor, American Church History, The Divinity School of Vanderbilt University, Nashville, Tennessee.

THE AMERICAN RELIGIOUS DEPRESSION 1925-1935
by Robert T. Handy

A distinguished professor of religious history identifies in this essay a significant "decade of depression" which marked a turning point in American Christianity. The religious depression, while certainly related to the economic depression, is distinguishable from it and in fact, Professor Handy argues, pre-dates it. This low period in spiritual morale was characterized by falling church attendance, a slump in missionary enthusiasm and social-gospel activism, the rise of scientism, behaviorism, and humanism as rivals to traditional theology, and the waning of a long-standing identification of Protestantism with American culture. The failure of Protestant nerve led to a loss of privileged position, the mushrooming of the sects, the rapid decline of liberal theology, and a preparation for Protestant renewal during the next three decades.

This thorough analysis of a limited but crucial period is a model of historical precision in exploring relations between religion and its social context.

For other titles in this series see last page.

FORTRESS PRESS
PHILADELPHIA, PA. 19129

85c